FOR OFFICIAL USE ONLY. **REVISED**

NOTES ON GUNNERY

FOR

DEFENSIVELY ARMED MERCHANT VESSELS,

Trawlers and Drifters.

R.N. GUNNERY SCHOOL,
CHATHAM.

Jan., 1918.

The Naval & Military Press Ltd

Published by

The Naval & Military Press Ltd
Unit 5 Riverside, Brambleside,
Bellbrook Industrial Estate,
Uckfield, East Sussex,
TN22 1QQ England

Tel: +44 (0) 1825 749494
Fax: +44 (0) 1825 765701

www.naval-military-press.com
www.nmarchive.com

The Library & Archives Department at the Royal Armouries Museum, Leeds, specialises in the history and development of armour and weapons from earliest times to the present day. Material relating to the development of artillery and modern fortifications is held at the Royal Armouries Museum, Fort Nelson.

For further information contact:
Royal Armouries Museum, Library, Armouries Drive, Leeds, West Yorkshire LS10 1LT
Royal Armouries, Library, Fort Nelson, Down End Road, Fareham PO17 6AN

Or visit the Museum's website at
www.armouries.org.uk

In reprinting in facsimile from the original, any imperfections are inevitably reproduced and the quality may fall short of modern type and cartographic standards.

CONTENTS.

I.—General Instructions.
Procedure when in Port.
Procedure when in Submarine Waters.

II.—Instructions for Drill and Practice.
Suggested Daily Routine.

III.—Sighting.
Easy Theory.
Telescopes—Description.
 —Illumination of.
Sight-setting.
Dial Lamps.

IV.—Care and Maintenance.
Ammunition in ready supply.
Mounting and Gun.
Sights.
Telescopes.

Tests before Practice Firing.

V.—Drill for all Guns.

VI.—Single Gun Control.

VII.—Single Gun Anti-Aircraft Control.

VIII.—Ammunition.

IX.—Hints on Shooting.

X.—Notes on the Submarine.

I.—GENERAL INSTRUCTIONS.

The ratings embarked are entirely responsible for the efficiency in all respects of the gun and ammunition, which should be ready day and night. One of the ratings is to act as Gunlayer, and the other as Breechworker. The senior rating is to arrange with the master as to detailing :—

(a) The necessary additional men to complete the gun's crew up to the numbers laid down.

(b) A sufficient number of hands over and above the gun's crew to supply ammunition to the gun in action.

All these hands should receive instruction in their duties from the senior rating as soon as possible after they join the ship.

The standard drill can be found in this book (page 16) and the number of men required at each type of gun is :—

	Gunlay'r	Trainer	B. Worker	Rammer	Proj.	Cart.	Sight Setter.
6in.	1	1	1	1	2	2	1
4·7in.	1	1	1	1	1	1	1
4in.	1	1	1	1	1	1	1
15 pdr.							
13 pdr.							
12 pdr.							
6 pdr.	1	1*	1		1	1	1
3 pdr. (Hots.)							
3 pdr. (Vickers)							
3in. (H.A.)							

*Only for guns fitted with separate training gear.

(*See Confidential Addenda 1*).

PROCEDURE WHILE THE VESSEL IS IN PORT.—The master should arrange whenever possible that the space in the immediate vicinity of the gun is railed off, and passengers and other unauthorised persons should not be allowed near the gun. A notice to this effect should be posted up near the gun.

2. One of the two ratings is always to be on board to keep guard on the gun and ammunition, and the master is to use his discretion as to keeping both ratings on board, should he consider such a course desirable.

3. The gun is to be kept covered at all times when not in use.

4. Whenever anchored in the vicinity of a British man-of-war, a request should be made to the Commanding Officer of the man-of-war for an armourer to inspect the gun and mounting.

At most ports there is now a R.N.R. Officer called an Officer Instructor. He is an Officer with special training whose duty is to look after D.A.M.S. while in that Port, and to give the guns' crews a rub up.

5. The gun's crew are to be specially warned that the gun is on no account to be loaded when the ship is in harbour.

The ship's magazines are to be kept locked.

On arrival in harbour the portable magazine is to be removed from the hold and the ammunition taken out and placed under lock and key in the ship's permanent magazine.

A fire hose is to be kept rigged in the immediate vicinity, also a bucket of sand.

When the holds are stowed the ammunition is once more to be placed in the portable magazine.

The portable magazine, when stowed, is to be easy of access in case of fire, and a fire hose is to be kept rigged and led to it.

PROCEDURE WHEN IN SUBMARINE WATERS.—When in submarine waters everything should be in a state of readiness, but the gun should not be kept actually loaded.

Percussion firing should always be used as it is the most certain way of discharging the gun, and therefore a ready supply of 10 complete rounds with *percussion* tubes in the cartridges is to be kept at the gun day and night.

- NOTE. (*a*) The present allowance of percussion tubes is only *one* per cartridge. Care should be taken that this supply of percussion tubes is kept aside for *action* and never used for *practice firing*.

- NOTE. (*b*) Cartridges in ready supply are the only ones which should be kept tubed. Other tubes should be kept in their sealed boxes to preserve them from damage and damp.

- NOTE. (*c*) Should the supply of percussion tubes give out, electric firing would have to be adopted: hence all electric firing mechanism and batteries must be kept efficient in every respect.

In *daytime* one of the trained ratings should be at the gun as a look-out, and the other rating handy.

At *night* one rating should be on watch, and sufficient men to fight the gun sleeping near by. (Some sort of alarm should be fitted from the bridge).

ACTION.—The master is responsible for handling the ship and for opening and ceasing fire, and may possibly decide to control the fire himself or he may detail an officer to carry out this duty. G.L'.s must be prepared for this and must remember that in controlled fire, their duty is only to lay and fire the gun and not to interfere in any way with the sights.

The master will probably keep the submarine astern, so that little deflection will be necessary, and the range will probably not be changing very rapidly.

The point of aim should be the centre of the submarine at the water line.

(See Confidential Addenda 2)

Notes on control and spotting are given on page 20 of this book, and should be learnt by heart and applied in action.

The firing should be "deliberate" until a hit is obtained when Independent Firing should be used for a few rounds (say 5 rounds).

At long ranges the rate of fire should be slower and more deliberate than at short ranges, as the shooting cannot be so accurate at long ranges, and the supply of ammunition may fail before a hit is obtained.

Remember—the main thing is to sink or cripple the submarine, or drive her off, and these notes are only to be taken as a help.

There must be perfect understanding between the master and the gun's crew.

II.—INSTRUCTIONS FOR DRILL AND PRACTICES.

As soon as possible after joining, the senior rating should arrange with the Master to take the gun's crew and supply party at drill (as laid down in this book) as often as possible until proficient, and then periodically.

Aiming practice with percussion firing gear should be carried out daily, the Gunlayer keeping the gun laid on the horizion and firing *without* tube or ammunition in the gun, the breech worker going through the motions of opening the breech, cocking the lock, closing the breech, and reporting "Ready." The striker should not be actually cocked and released unless there is a drill cartridge in the gun as constant snapping of the striker without a cartridge may fracture the firing pin. In guns fitted with training gear the trainer should also be exercised with the G.L., whenever a suitable object presents itself.

Gunlayers will find that, with any motion on the ship, laying on the horizon is not at all an easy matter, and constant daily practice for about fifteen minutes at the simple aiming drill will accustom them to the guns and "keep their eye in,"

Aiming rifle practice should also be constantly carried out, care being taken that the range is clear. The rifle supplied for this purpose should be lashed to the side of the gun, arrangements being made if practicable for the rifle to be fired by a lanyard lead to the proper firing lever of the gun.

A box or other suitable object should be dropped as a target and fire opened at a range of about 500 yards, and continued until the splash of the shot can no longer be seen.

The ammunition expended in this way is limited to 50 rounds a day, and not more than 150 rounds a month.

(See Confidential Addenda 3).

ALL TESTS BEFORE FIRING (pages 13 and 14) are to be carefully carried out before practice firing, with full calibre ammunition.

During practice firing, the drill as laid down (page 16) must be properly carried out.

SUGGESTED DAILY ROUTINE.—

- a.m. Sponge out—Clean gun.—Lubricate all parts.—See everything working easily.—Gunlayer practice laying on horizon.—Sight-setter and Breech-worker also at drill.
- p.m. Clean gun.—Test night sights and dial lamps.—See everything working easily.—Inspect ready supply of ammunition to see everything is ready for the night.

III.—SIGHTS.

EASY THEORY.—The projectile travels in a curve between the gun and the target. To make the projectile travel further we have to raise the muzzle of the gun. We do this by first of all lowering the telescope (without moving the gun), and to bring the telescope up on to the object again, we raise the gun and hence put on the extra elevation.

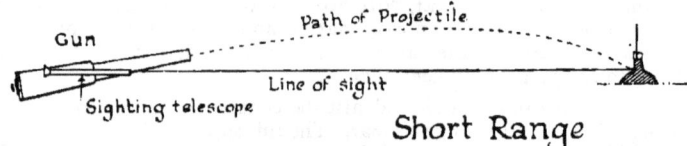

Short Range

Similarly, to make the shot fall more to the right, we put on Right Deflection, which moves the telescope to the left, without altering the gun. The gun has then to be trained right to get telescope on again, and hence the shot pitches more to the right.

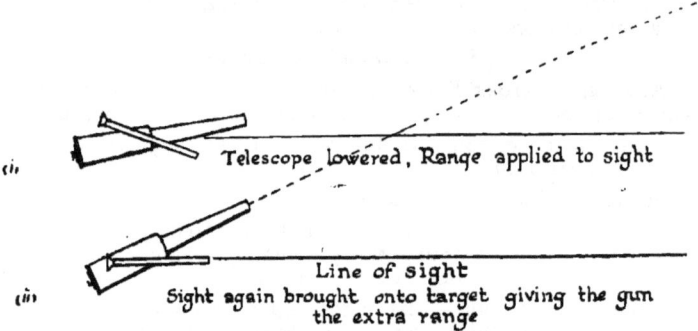

Long Range

With the Tangent Sight, i.e., the sight used in some 15-pdrs. and 3-pdrs., the foresight is fixed to the gun, and so to make the shot travel further, i.e., to put more elevation on the gun, the back sight is raised. To get the sights aligned on the target we must again raise the gun, and this gives the extra elevation required.

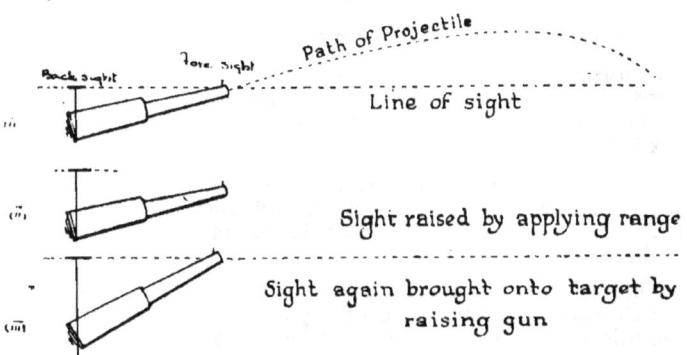

For care and maintenance see page 12.

TELESCOPES.—Can be altered (1) for focus, (2) for power.
The choice of power depends on :—

(*a*). BRIGHTNESS OF DAY.—On a bright day a high power can be used. As the power of a telescope is increased, so the light in the telescope is diminished ; consequently on a dull day, a lower power should be used, as the target will not be so easily seen if a high power is used.

(*b*). MOTION ON THE SHIP.—This is a question of "Field of View." When much motion is on the ship, it is necessary to have a large field of view, so that the object can be kept in sight the whole time, consequently a low power is necessary.

If there is little or no motion on the ship a high power can be employed, as the gunlayer does not require such a large field of view.

TO FOCUS A TELESCOPE :—(1). Set telescope at the lowest power and focus until the object is clearly seen.

(2). Gradually increase the power until brilliancy begins to decrease.

The cap supplied for the object glass of the telescope is seldom of use except when spray is coming over or when firing in a strong glare.

For care and maintenance, see page 13.

ILLUMINATION OF TELESCOPES.—For night work a small lamp is fitted for illuminating the cross wires. The cross wires should only be showing faintly, and to adjust their brilliance a small resistance box is included in the circuit.

TO ADJUST:—Switch full on, and then by turning the milled head of the resistance box decrease the brilliancy till correct. Take out the peg and screw it into the hole next to the correct position of the switch.

The peg will then act as a stop, at the correct position of the switch when switching on in a hurry in the dark. Under normal conditions the lamp should be switched to OFF as soon as the peg has been adjusted, otherwise the lamps will soon get worn out.

SIGHTSETTING.—If the senior rating has to train a sightsetter, he should go about it in the same way as he himself was taught in the school. Even if he has a trained sightsetter, he should keep him up to the mark by giving him frequent exercises of the following nature (both during the day and the night.

Range and deflection at commencement of run:—

```
                        3800 yds.                16 Right.
              (i.)   Down  1600 yds..............Right 10
Spotting      (ii.)  Up     400  ,, ...............  ,,    2
Corrections   (iii.)  ,,    400  ,, ...............       —
              (iv.)  Down   200  ,, ...............Left   4
                     Result 2800 yds.            24 Right.
```

It is most essential to good shooting that spotting corrections are put on accurately and quickly.

DIAL LAMPS.—For illuminating the sight dials at night, small dial lamps are provided, fed from a battery. These should only be switched on on testing through at night to see that they are correct for night action. If the lamps are left burning, the batteries will run down, and the lamps will get worn out.

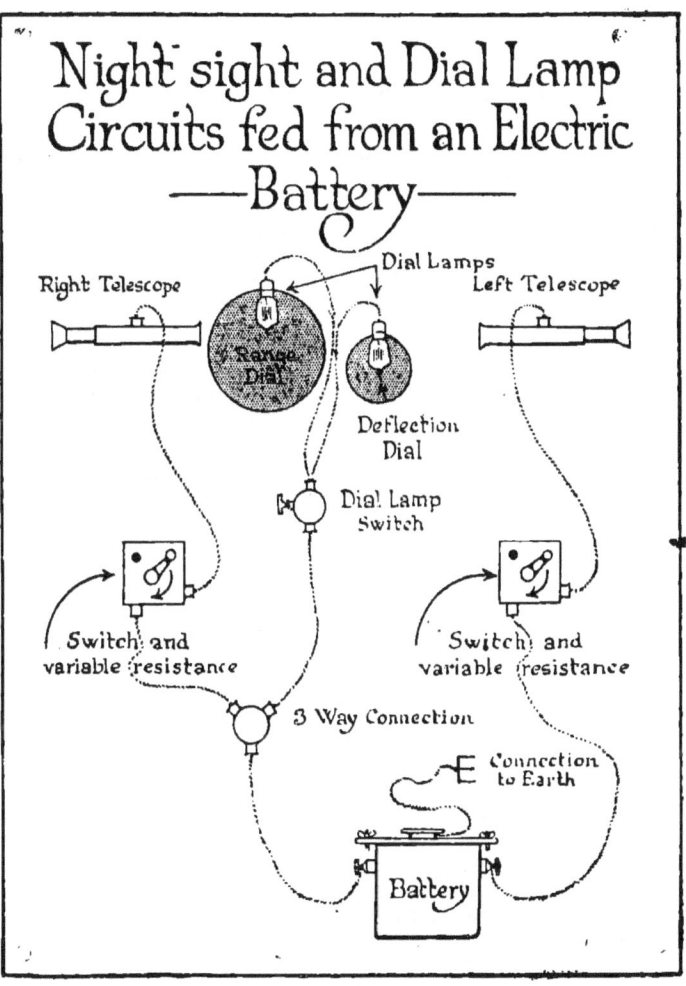

IV.—CARE AND MAINTENANCE.

CARE AND MAINTENANCE (GENERAL).—Great attention is to be paid to the ready supply of ammunition, to keep it clean and dry.

If *tubes and cartridges* are not kept dry there is considerable danger of hanging fire, i.e., the charge smouldering instead of going off at once, and then perhaps going off some appreciable time after the trigger is pressed.

In case the cartridges are suspected of being wet, they should be laid aside until return to harbour, when the local Officer should be informed at once.

The *Projectiles* are to be lightly oiled.

When the weather is frosty the gun and ammunition should be covered with canvas or tarpaulin, to prevent them from becoming frozen, but the covering should be such as not to interfere in any way with readiness for action.

For the maintenance of the gun and mounting, it is to be borne in mind that "*Lubrication is the secret of efficiency in gun machinery.*"

It is to be remembered that *vaseline* is a preservative only.

Oil is a *lubricant*.

Each morning and evening the following is to be carried out :—

(1) See that the bore is clear.

(2) See that the recoil cylinders are full (page 13).

(3) Gauge the protrusion of the striker (page 14).

(4) Train and elevate the gun to the extremes of training and elevation, and see that everything works smoothly.

(5) Run the sights up and down to the extremes of the range, and across to the extremes of Right and Left Deflection, and see they work smoothly.

In the evening the *Telescope Illuminating Lamps* should be switched on, and the brilliancy of the cross wires adjusted. The *Dial Lamps* also should be switched on to see they are burning correctly, then *all* lamps should be switched off.

The gun is to be cleaned twice a day, cleaning gear being supplied by the Master.

The bore should be kept clean and slightly oiled.

Brick dust is not to be used on machined surfaces.

At the same time all the working parts should be well lubricated, and all oil holes, pipes, and channels, kept perfectly clear and free for the passage of the lubricant, especially to the following parts :—

(1) Trunnions.
(2) Elevating gear.
(3) Training worm and worm wheel.
(4) Ball race (if fitted).
(5) Pivot.
(6) Inside of cradle.
(7) Sights.
(8) Breech mechanism.

CARE OF SIGHTS.—Sights are to be kept clean, free from grit, and oiled.

No brick dust is to be used on sights.

CARE OF TELESCOPES.—Silk cloth should be provided for cleaning the glasses of Telescopes.

It should be remembered that gun sighting Telescopes are extremely delicate optical instruments, and they are *on no account* to be parted, or the lenses removed.

They should be handled very carefully.

Remember—if Telescopes get out of order, the open sights (fitted in most guns) can be used.

TESTS BEFORE PRACTICE FIRING.

(1) See the recoil cylinders and tanks are filled. This is very important, as there will be a serious accident if the recoil cylinders are not properly filled. There will then be nothing to absorb the recoil of the gun.

WHEN CYLINDER IS EMPTY.—Method of filling.—The recoil cylinders are filled with a mixture consisting of half water and half glycerine. The general procedure is to give the gun full depression.

Ease back the drain plug, unscrew the filling plug and air plug. Fill through the filling plug and as soon as liquid starts to trickle out through the drain plug, screw it up tightly. Carry on filling till the liquid comes out of the air plug, then screw that up, and fill to the top of the filling plug. Then screw up the filling plug.

FOR DAILY INSPECTION (after the cylinder is once filled).—It is not necessary to take out the drain plug. Place the gun at max. depression. Just take out the filling plug, and ease off the air plug until liquid starts to come out at air plug, then screw up the air plug, and fill up at filling plug, then screw up the filling plug.

(Special instructions are given for mountings where these three plugs are not fitted).

(2) See that the bore is clear.

(3) Remove any moveable objects in the way of the blast from the gun.

(4) The striker is to be examined to see—

(a) That sheath nut is screwed up and keep pin in place and intact.

(b) That needle set and check nuts are screwed up.

(c) That striker does not protrude [with the B.M. lever in the open position.

(d) That striker does not move forward till marks on breech block and gun are in line.

(e) That safety stop is correct and keep screw is in place (6 and 4in. Q.F. and 12-pdr.)

(5) The striker is to be gauged.

This is carried out in the following manner :—

Open the breech, press in on the catch, retaining breech screw open, and close the B.M. lever, at the same time holding on to the carrier to prevent the latter closing. The striker is now protruding, and can be gauged with the gauge supplied. When the striker is bearing on the face A the face CC should be clear of the face of the breech screw (see fig. 1).

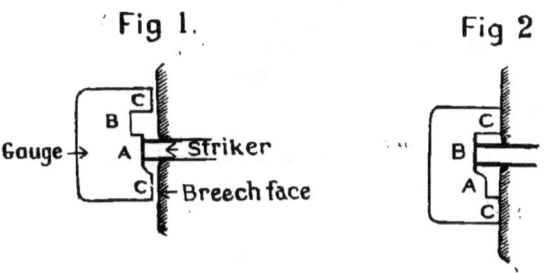

When the face of the breech screw is bearing on CC the striker should be clear of the face B (See fig. 2).

If the striker is protruding too much it will strike the tube as the breech is swung to (if No. 2 has forgotten to cock the striker), and fire the gun before the breech is properly closed.

Procedure if there is too little protrusion :—

Renew leather washer under the head of the needle, putting in a thicker one. Should this be insufficient, the firing pin or needle should be replaced.

If the striker is not protruding enough, it will never touch the tube when the striker is released, and there will be a missfire.

Procedure if there is too much protrusion :—

Rub down the leather washer under the head of the needle with a piece of glass paper, thus making it thinner. Should this be insufficient, the firing pin or needle should be replaced.

NOTE :—In guns fitted with "A" Breech mechanism, the mechanism is never to be taken apart and clauses (*a*), (*b*) and (*e*) of the last paragraph do not apply, but the following should be seen to :—

(1) The nut retaining striker must be seen screwed up and keep-screw in place.

(2) In percussion firing the breech worker should see that the sear is set for percussion firing, and that the striker is retained to the rear on lowering the cam lever.

V.—DRILL.

DRILL.—The following drill is to be carried out at all guns (except where a special gun is referred to).

PRELIMINARY DRILL.—Dress and number the class.

Detail off the gun's crew (see page 3).

Instruct each number in his duties.

Position of the gun's crew " Closed up."

,, ,, ,, " Fallen out."

Method of " changing round."

Teach " Still " and " Rest."

Quick Time   *Procedure.*

Cast Loose.

All numbers clear away obstructions.

G.L. Trains clear.

2 opens the breech, examines it and the striker (and sees that striker does not protrude with the breech open.)

3 removes the tampeon.

G.L. reports " Bore clear."

2 closes the breech (and then for guns firing " separate " ammunition, provides percussion tubes and hand extractor).

G.L. provides and ships the telescopes.

S.S. runs sights through full limits of elevation and deflection.

Loaders clear away the supply and provide 10 rounds, inserting the percussion tubes in the cartridges.

When a loading tray is not fitted to the mounting No. 3 provides loading tray (where supplied).

NOTE :—This is termed the cleared away position.

17

Action.
> Gun's crew close up at the gun.
>
> G.L. reports bore clear.
>
> Magazine party and supply party proceed to magazine and supplies.
>
> Captain of gun orders "Load."
>
> 2 opens the breech and cocks the striker.
>
> Loaders insert projectile and cartridge with tube in it. (3 working the loading tray at guns not fitted with a permanent loading tray).
>
> At guns fitted with a B.M. lever, 2 closes the breech then withdraws the B.M. lever, and reports "Half cock."

Load.
> *At 3-pdr. Semi-Auto.*
>
> 2 closes breech, puts safety lever to "Half cock" and reports "Half cock."
>
> *At 3 and 6pdr. Hotchkiss.*
>
> 2 keeps the breech lowered.

Object.
When the object is named, the gun is trained on the object. S.S. adjusts the sights as ordered and reports "Set."

Ready
When trained on the object, Captain of the gun orders "Ready."

2 closes the breech or puts safety lever to "fire," or hooks on the firing lanyard (as necessary), steps clear and reports "ready."

18

Fire.

When ordered to open fire by the Captain of the ship or as previously arranged, Captain of the gun orders "Fire."

G.L. Fires

The gun is reloaded and brought to the ready.

Spotttng correction is given and S.S. reports "set."
Firing is continued either under the orders of the control officer, Captain of the gun, or G.L. fires "Independently."

Load with Lyddite or High Explosive.

As for "Load," but the number placing the projectile in the gun removes the pin and cap from the fuze, and reports "Pin out, cap off."

NOTE.—Pins and caps are not to be removed at other times; any shell which has had its pin and cap removed should have them carefully replaced before being restowed.

Cease Fire

G.L. discontinues the firing, and removes his finger from the trigger.

2 opens the breech carefully and withdraws the cartridge, and hands it to one of the loading numbers.

Unload and Secure.

The projectile in the gun, if base fuzed, is ejected and returned.

NOTE :—If loaded with a nose-fuzed shell, the gun must be discharged, as nose-fuzed shell are not to be ejected.

All numbers return the gear they provided.

Loading numbers fill up the ready supply rack, and return the remainder of the cartridges and projectiles to the magazine.

NOTE.—Care must be taken that tubes are taken out of the cartridges and returned to the magazine.

The G.L. trains the gun to the securing position and secures it. He then carefully unships and returns the telescopes.

NOTE.—Percussion tubes are always used until all the percussion tubes are finished. A ready supply of 10 Rounds always to be kept at the gun, night and day when at sea.

The tubes are always to be kept in the ready supply.

The gun is never to be kept loaded unless a submarine is actually in sight, or known to be in the immediate neighbourhood.

MISSFIRES.—If a missfire occurs with a percussion tube when in action, the following procedure is to be adopted by the breech worker:—

(1) On receiving the Gunlayer's order "missfire," tap the B.M. lever (or crank handle) to ensure the breech is properly closed.

(2) Then recock the striker.

If the gun again fails to fire, remove the striker and examine it to ensure the firing pin is not broken.

If the striker is unbroken, the breech is to be opened and the cartridge removed and thrown overboard, having first ascertained that there was a tube in the cartridge.

The gun is then to be reloaded and the firing continued.

Note :—When carrying out *Practice Firing* and a missfire occurs the breech mechanism is not to be moved until the following periods have elapsed.

12-pdr. and above (except 13-pdr.)	30 minutes.
13-pdr.	15 ,,
Below 12-pdr. ...	15 ,,

Casualties.—The Officer in charge (or the Captain of the gun in his absence) should provide for every contingency for filling up casualties which may occur.

It must be borne in mind that the gun must be fought so long as one man remains.

VI.—SINGLE GUN CONTROL AGAINST ENEMY SHIP OR SUBMARINE.

Note :—The remarks on Control in this section are simply to be taken as a general explanation of the "bracket" system, and in no way cancel Confidential Addenda 1.

Definitions :—

The "Range" is the distance in yards to the enemy.

The "Rate" or "Rate of change of Range" is the speed, usually in yards per minute, that the range is altering due to the difference in course and speed between our own ship and the enemy.

The efficient control of a single gun is a difficult matter for the following reasons :—

(1) There is no "spread" in which to include the target.

(2) Any "bad shot," *unless reported*, will give the spotter a wrong impression, But in order to make the utmost use of every shot, it is permissible to give a spotting correction under certain circumstances, e.g :—

G. Ls. report.	Fall of shot.	Procedure.
1 Bad Shot High.	Over.	No correction.
2 Bad Shot High.	Right.	Apply spotting correction for Deflection.
3 Bad Shot High.	Short.	Continue Bracket.
4 Bad Shot Low.	Short and Left.	No Correction to Range Apply Deflection correction.
5 Bad Shot Low, Left.	Over and Right.	Apply corrections both for Range & Deflection

It is necessary to find the hitting range as quickly as possible, and some system must be devised for this, as the estimated initial range is unlikely to prove correct.

The best—in fact the only reliable—system, is known as the *Bracket System.*

The idea of this is to get two consecutive shots, one short and one over or vice versa, so that it is then known that the enemy's range is somewhere between these two.

For instance, if the first round is fired with 1600 yards on the sights, and goes short, and the second shot fired with 2000 yards on, goes over, it is obvious that the range of the enemy lies between 1600 and 2000 yards. The correction should therefore be "Down 200"—i.e., halving the orginal bracket of 400 yards, and so on.

In order to find the range quickly a bracket should be used large enough to ensure that two consecutive shots fall on the opposite sides of the target.

It is important to get the first shot to fall OVER the submarine as it then shows her that the ship is able to reach her with her gun. The Range should therefore always be over-estimated rather than the reverse.

Having opened fire with estimated range, a preliminary correction of UP or DOWN 1600 should at once be given if it is obvious that the shot is a long way short or over.

Having corrected the fall of shot for Deflection an 800 or 400 yard bracket should be employed. The choice of the bracket depends on the range and the general conditions but the 400 yard bracket should not be used at ranges greater than about 2000 yards.

(*See Confidential Addenda 2*).

It is a simple method to find the correct range by this method, *if the range is not changing* ; but in practice of course this is very rarely the case, and allowance must be made for the alteration in the range. From this it will be seen that if the enemy is closing, i.e., the range is *decreasing*, it is necessary to keep the shots, if anything, *short*, so that the enemy will run into the danger zone. On the contrary, if the enemy is getting further away, i.e., the range is *increasing*, the shots, if anything, should be *over* for the same reason.

It should be remembered that with two ships closing or opening one another at a speed of 6 knots, the range will alter 200 yards a minute.

Two cases of Rate require to be dealt with :—
(*a*) Where it is obvious from the start that the range is Opening or Closing.

(*b*) Where this cannot be ascertained for certain.

Case (*a*). The Rate should be allowed for as soon as the Enemy has been crossed with a spotting correction of 400 yards or less.

Examples of rate to be allowed for :—

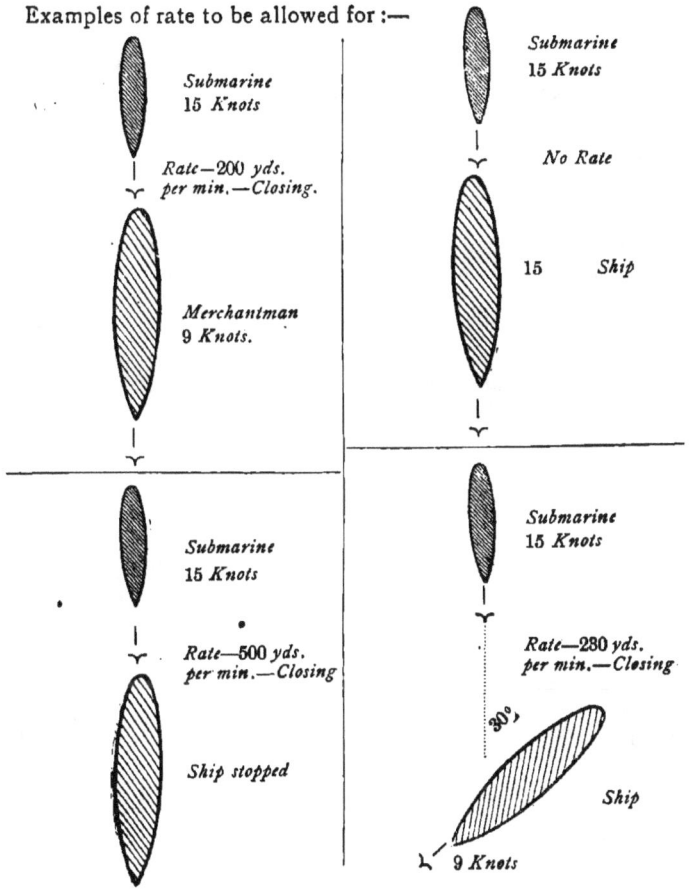

Wi the aid of the above examples it should be possible to estimate the rate with a certain degree of accuracy. Having estimated the rate and knowing the number of rounds that the gun is likely to fire a minute, it can easily be determined what spotting correction should be allowed for rate between each round.

E.G.—Estimated rate 300 yards per min.:

Rate of fire 3 rounds per min.:

Correction to be applied between shots—Down 100.

When applying a correction for rate at same time as bracketing think of the bracket correction first and then add to or subtract from it according to rate.

Case (*b*). No allowance should be made for rate until the bracket has been worked out to the end or a hit obtained. If, after hitting has commenced, it is definitely seen that the shots are starting to draw short or over (all shots being good shots) it is obvious that there must be an opening or closing rate and this must then be at once allowed for by spotting corrections as before.

No spotting correction of less than 100 yards should ever be given at ranges greater than about 2000 yards and in NO case should a correction of less than 50 yards be given.

DEFLECTION.—The Deflection is the correction that must be put on the sights to bring the shot from the Right or Left on to the target. The Deflection to be put on the sights must allow for the following :—

(1) Speed of your own ship.

(2) Speed of enemy.

(3) Wind.

(1) SPEED OF YOUR OWN SHIP. The shot, as it leaves the gun, is travelling along with the gun, and the gun is moving along with the ship. Hence the shot has a movement in the direction in which your own ship is moving. To counteract this, deflection must be applied in the *opposite direction* to the ship's course.

The *amount* of deflection to be applied to counteract this cause, is a maximum when firing on the beam, and decreases to nothing when firing right ahead or right astern.

As a rough guide allow the following :—

(1) Enemy on the beam—number of knots ship is steaming.

(2) Enemy 60° from the beam— half the number of knots ship is steaming.

(3) Enemy ahead or astern—Nil.

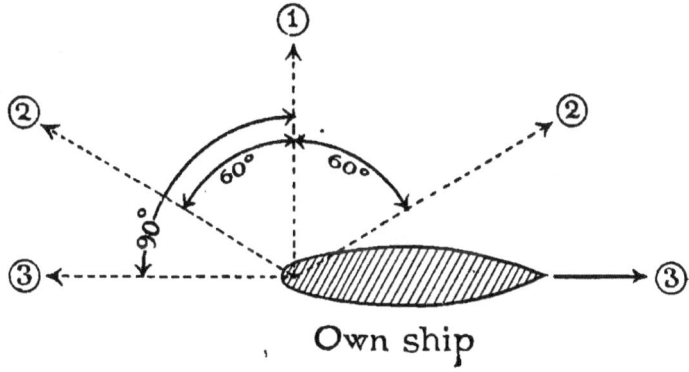

(2) SPEED OF ENEMY. It is obvious that if you fire straight at an enemy which is moving, by the time the shot has reached the

enemy, she will have moved out of the way. To counteract this, deflection must be put on the sights in the *same direction* as that in which the enemy is steaming.

The amount of deflection to be applied to counteract this movement of the enemy is a maximum when the enemy is steaming at right angles to the line of fire, and decreases to nothing when she is steaming along the line of fire, i.e., straight towards or straight away from you. As a rough guide allow the following :—

(1) Enemy steaming at right angles to line of fire :—
   Allow number of knots you think she is steaming.

(2) Enemy steaming at 30° to line of fire :—
   Allow half number of knots you think she is steaming.

(3) Enemy coming straight towards you or going straight away :—
   Allow nothing.

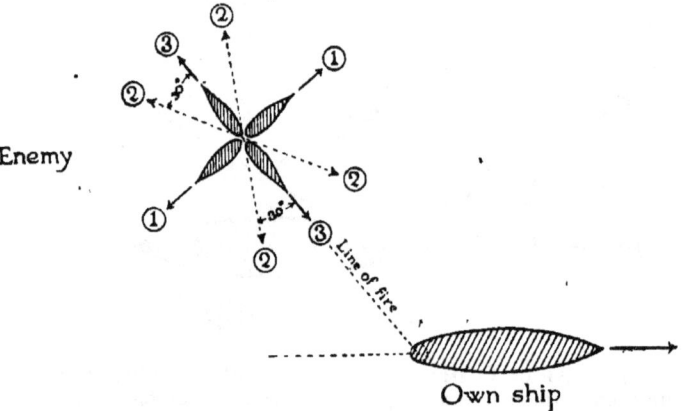

(3) WIND. If a strong wind is blowing, the shot will be blown away down wind.

To counteract this, deflection must be put on the sight to bring the shot up to windward, i.e., the *direction of the deflection* must be the direction *from which the wind is blowing*.

The *amount* of deflection necessary to counteract the effect of the wind must be estimated according to the force of the wind across the line of fire.

At short ranges (i.e., under 2,000 yards) this should not be large, unless the wind is very strong.

POINT OF AIM.—If it is required to hit some point other than that aimed at, deflection must be put on the sights to achieve this. This deflection is allowed in the direction in which the projectile is required to fall, i.e., if the point to be hit is to the left of the point of aim, left deflection is required and vice versa.

In firing at a submarine the point of aim will probably coincide with the point to be hit, as both will no doubt be the conning tower or periscope. Therefore correction for point of aim does not come in.

In practice therefore when the enemy is sighted, a rough calculation should be made. Thus:

(1) Enemy is astern—Deflection due to own speed ... 0

Enemy is coming straight at us. } —Deflection due to enemy .. 0

Strong wind on the Port beam. } —Deflection due to wind—6 kts. right.

Total - 6 Right.

This total should be put on the sights.

28

Enemy.   *Own Ship.*

Or another case :—

(2) Own speed 9 knots and Enemy's speed 15 knots.

    Enemy on the port beam—Deflection due to own speed   9 Left.

    Enemy steering on same course as ourselves—Deflection due to enemy   15 Right.

    Strong wind on the Port beam— Deflection due to wind   0

                                                 Total - 6 Right.

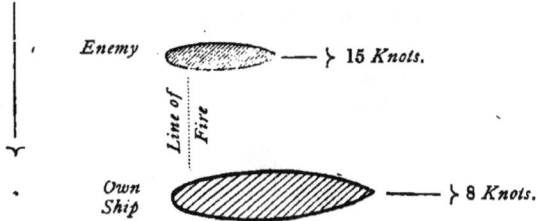

After firing the first shot the correction for deflection must be in the direction in which the projectile is required to fall (i.e., if the shot falls to the left the correction is " Right so much," and vice versa).

It is necessary in all cases to correct for deflection before commencing the Range bracket.

This does NOT mean that the deflection must be ABSOLUTELY correct before starting the range bracket; as soon as the shot falls near enough to the Enemy for line to enable the G.L. or spotting Officer to determine for CERTAIN whether it is Over or Short, the range bracket should at once be commenced.

Further necessary corrections to the deflection can then be applied during the working of the range bracket.

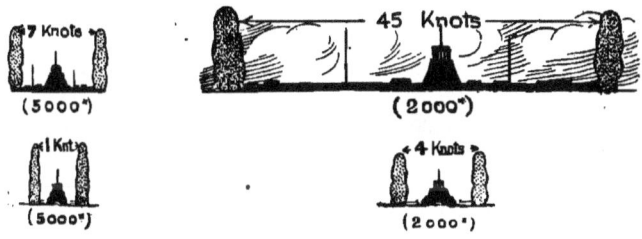

Until correct for line, bold spotting corrections for deflections are absolutely necessary. No correction of less than 10 knots should be given when the shot falls clear of the enemy. It will make the work of the S.S. easier if even numbers are always used for deflection and no correction of less than two knots should be necessary except when HITTING a submarine end on.

Method of communicating Range and Deflection, and Orders.

Ranges :—

(a) All figures in the range to be called.

(b) "O" to be called "Oh."

(c) When the same figures occur twice in succession, they are to be called "double—," as in the telephone system, except in the case of exact thousands.

(d) The words "thousand" and "hundred" to be omitted.

Thus :—Two five double oh	2500
Three thousand	3000
Double two double oh	2200

Spotting Orders for Range.—To distinguish these from actual Ranges :—

(a) The word "up" or "down" is to precede the amount.

(b) The amount of the spotting order is to be passed in words, and not in figures.

(c) The word "yards" is to be omitted.

Thus:—"Up two hundred."

DEFLECTION.—Each figure is to be called separately:

    Thus:—One oh right   10 Right.

    Double two right   22 Right.

SPOTTING ORDERS FOR DEFLECTION.—To distinguish these from actual Deflections the word "Right" or "Left" is to precede the amount, and the amount is to be passed in words.

Thus:—"Right Twelve"—Come twelve more knots to the right of your present deflection.

THE BEARING OF THE ENEMY is passed to the gun with reference to bow, beam or quarter, and on the port or starboard side.

SPECIMEN RUNS (1).—Enemy speed 10 knots, bearing astern.

Own ship speed 10 knots. No wind.

In this simple case the Range is not changing, and there is no deflection.

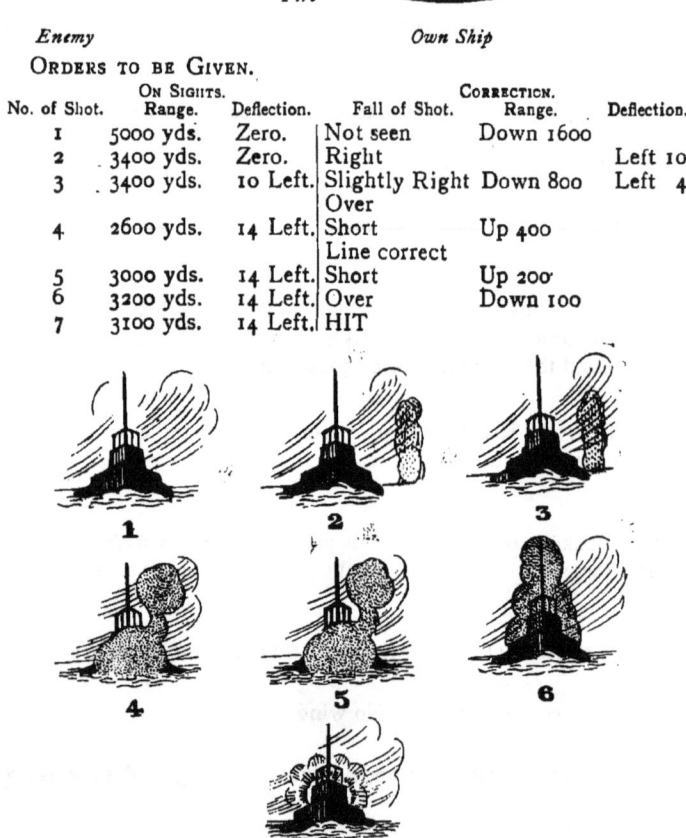

Enemy   *Own Ship*

ORDERS TO BE GIVEN.

No. of Shot.	On Sights. Range.	Deflection.	Fall of Shot.	Correction. Range.	Deflection.
1	5000 yds.	Zero.	Not seen	Down 1600	
2	3400 yds.	Zero.	Right		Left 10
3	3400 yds.	10 Left.	Slightly Right Over	Down 800	Left 4
4	2600 yds.	14 Left.	Short Line correct	Up 400	
5	3000 yds.	14 Left.	Short	Up 200	
6	3200 yds.	14 Left.	Over	Down 100	
7	3100 yds.	14 Left.	HIT		

SPECIMEN RUN (2).—Enemy 15 knots bearing on the quarter.
Course parallel to own course.
Own ship 8 knots. No Wind.

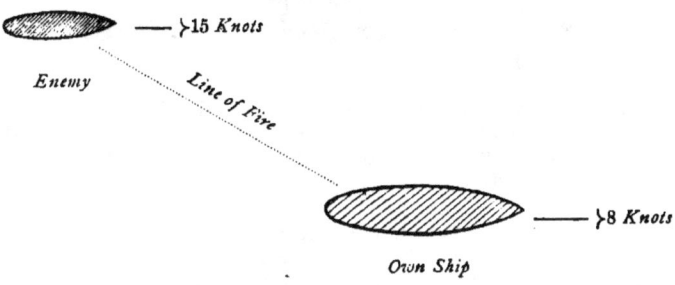

	ON SIGHTS.		CORRECTION.		
No of Shot	Range.	Deflection.	Fall of Shot.	Range.	Deflection.
1	Max. elev.	4 Right	Left		Right 10
2	Max. elev.	14 ,,	Over Right	Down 800	Left 4
3	5,200 yds.	10 ,,	Over Line correct	Down 800	
4	4,400 yds.	10 ,,	Short Left edge	Up 400	Right 2 "B.S.H."
5	4,800 yds.	12 ,,	Over	Down 200 Down 100	
6	4,500 yds.	12 ,,	HIT	Down 100	

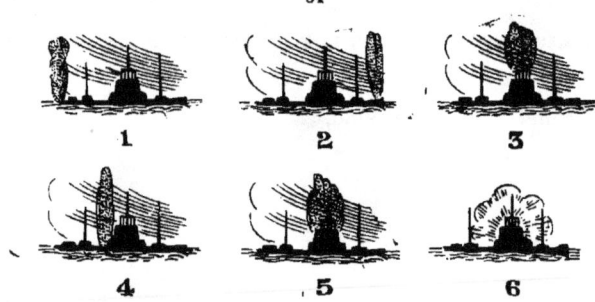

The above example shows the case where the Control Officer or G.L. realises from the commencement that there is a closing rate and starts to allow for it as soon as he has crossed the Enemy with a 400 yard correction.

Had it been a case where it was impossible to judge whether the rate was Opening or Closing the Control Officer or G.L. would have waited until he had worked the bracket out to 100 yards and then, failing to get a hit afterwards he would have allowed for rate as follows, e.g.—

5	4800	12 R :	Over	Down 200	
6	4600	12 R :	Over	Down 100	
7	4500	12 R :	Over	No correction	
8	4500	12 R :	Over	Down 200	
9	4300	12 R :	Short Left edge	No correction	Right 2
10	4300	14 R :	Hit	Down 100	

In the above example the G.L. was justified in hoping that his 7th shot would have hit had there been no rate and he therefore fired the 8th shot with the same range on the sights to make quite certain. As the 8th shot also fell over and was a "good shot" the G.L. came Down 200 as a first correction for rate. The next shot fell short and the G.L. made no alteration in the range as the Enemy was running into his shots. The 10th shot hit and the G.L. allowed for rate by coming Down 100.

Remember when in doubt start bracketing again.

NOTE :—In firing at an enemy ship or submarine at comparatively short range, *hits* will probably be seen, but at long range *hits* and *overs* may both be invisible, and it is then best to get an occasional short shot, to give some idea of where the shot is falling.

VII.—SINGLE GUN ANTI-AIRCRAFT CONTROL.

As aircraft fly at high speeds and can manoeuvre with great freedom, the chief point to bear in mind when controlling H.A. fire is that rapidity is all important.

There must be no hesitation in giving corrections and the fuze setting numbers of the Gun's crew must be drilled frequently, until they really can set fuzes quickly under all conditions.

There are two main types of A.A. Sight in use in Trawlers and Drifters :—

1. Older pattern sights such as Burns sight.
2. New pattern Sights.

1. These sights are usually complicated and have a large number of dials.

Burns Sight has the following :—

    Range.
    Deflection.
    Course of enemy.
    Speed of enemy.
    Vertical Deflection. (Not fitted to 6-pdr. Hotchkiss MK.IV)

RANGE is expressed in yards an usual.

DEFLECTION, on some sights is in knots, on others in degrees.

COURSE OF ENEMY in degrees. If the enemy is steering directly away from the gun, the course is said to be Zero. If directly towards—1800. If the enemy is crossing from Right to Left at Right angles to the line of fire, then his course is 90° to the Left, and so on.

SPEED OF ENEMY. Usually graduated in knots.

VERTICAL DEFLECTION. This should always be left set to Zero.

2. The Sight for 12-pdr. 12 cwt. Gun on Mark VIII. H.A. Mtg. is typical of the newer patterns.

This sight is a good deal simpler than the old type, and has the following dials :—

    Combined Range and Fuze strip.
    Vertical Deflection.
    Horizontal or " Cross " Deflection.

COMBINED RANGE and FUZE STRIP, contains Ranges in yards side by side with Fuze Settings for either No.84 or No. 65A fuzes.

The Sight can be used either for ranges or fuzes by setting a pointer opposite one of two marks on an arc. One mark being called " Air Fuzes " and the other " Ranges."

It should always be set opposite the Air Fuzes mark.

VERTICAL DEFLECTION Dial is graduated in degrees "Up" or "Down," and has a locking plate which can be used if desired to hold the dial in the Zero position.

HORIZONTAL DEFLECTION. This dial is labelled "cross" deflection and is graduated in degrees and knots Right and Left.

Degrees or knots may be used as desired by turning over the plate carrying the pointer for deflection.

Other patterns of later sights may have the Vertical Deflection and Range marked on two dials one on top of the other.

Some sights have the ordinary range and deflection dials only.

METHODS OF CONTROL :—

It must be remembered that it is most important to fire a round as soon as possible after sighting aircraft, which are known to be hostile, provided they are considered to be within range.

The reason for this is that it is very unlikely that the first estimate of Range, Deflection and Fuze will be correct and the only sure way of finding out is to get a burst in the air, and to correct the position of that burst.

In the case of guns not provided with time fuzed ammunition, it is advisable to wait until the aircraft is close enough for the track of the tracer to be followed.

The point of aim should be a standard one known to the Gun-layer beforehand, so that no time is lost on sighting the enemy. The most suitable point of aim is the bow.

ORDERS BEFORE OPENING FIRE.

Burns Sight.

- (a) Bearing and Nature of enemy.
- (b) Nature of shell, where necessary.
- (c) Range and Fuze setting.
- (d) Course and Speed of enemy.
- (e) "Control" and "Fire."

Remainder as in present book, pp. 5, 6, 7 and 8, omitting reference to point of aim and add in par. 3, Page 6, line 2, after "Range on Sights "—" obtained from Fuze Scale."

Newer Sights.

- (a) Bearing and Object.
- (b) Nature of projectile, where necessary.
- (c) Fuze setting.
- (d) Vertical and Cross Deflection.
- (e) "Control" and "Fire."

(c) In the case of aeroplanes the pilot as a general rule will not alter his height very considerably while under fire, and the best way of calculating the fuze to be used, is to assume a definite height for the aircraft, and to select a fuze according to the angle of Elevation of the enemy.

Allowance must be made for the alteration of position of the enemy during the time necessary between setting the fuzes and getting a burst in the air.

(d) Vertical Deflection must be allowed for according to whether the enemy is approaching or receding. If enemy is approaching and the line of sight is parallel to the bore of gun, it is obvious that, by the time the projectile gets from the gun to the point of bursting, the enemy will have moved on considerably.

By means of the Vertical Deflection dial it is possible to give the gun more or less elevation than the sight, so than by keeping the sight on the enemy the projectile will travel so as to meet the enemy at the end of its time of flight.

Vertical Deflection is Zero where the aircraft is crossing from Right to Left or vice versa, and a maximum when the enemy is coming straight towards or going straight away from the gun.

A good Deflection to open fire with on approaching or receding aircraft is 3° up or down respectively.

CROSS DEFLECTION is necessary for the same reasons as vertical deflection, only in this case it is a maximum when the aircraft is crossing from Right to Left or vice versa, and is Zero in the event of the enemy coming straight towards or going straight away from the gun.

Vertical and Cross deflection require alteration for every alteration in the course of the enemy, and also to bring the burst in line with the aircraft in the first instance.

SPECIMEN RUN.
 Bearing Red 45. an aeroplane.
 Lyddite Shell.
 Fuze 14.
 Up 3° Left 2°
 "Control" "Fire."

Burst appears Right and low. Left 2° Up 1°

Burst appears Short. Fuze 16. Etc.

It is important to remember that when the enemy is approaching the fuze must be continually reduced, and the vertical Deflection increased in the UP direction, and when receding the fuze must be lengthened and the Vertical Deflection put more DOWN.

VIII.—AMMUNITION.

CORDITE, of which all charges are composed, is highly imflamable and every precaution must be taken to guard against fire.

CARTRIDGES for Breech Loading guns are composed of cordite. For safety, convenience and rapidity in loading the cordite is placed in a silk cloth bag. The cordite sticks are tied in bundles with silk braid, and at one end of the bag is sewn a red shalloon bag containing the powder igniter. This igniter is to assist the ignition of the cordite and the charge must always be placed in the gun *with the Igniter to the rear*.

Q.F. charges are either :—

(1) Separate. I.e., projectile and cartridge are loaded separately into the gun, 4.7in., 4in., 12-pdr., &c., or (2) Fixed. I.e., projectile and cartridge are fixed together and loaded into the gun together 3, 6, & 13-pdr.

"SEPARATE AMMUNITION."—At the rear end of the silk cloth bag a space is left for a powder igniter which is secured to the charge.

The charge is placed into a brass cartridge case with the cordite cylinder and igniter covering an adaptor. The adaptor is secured to the brass cylinder and fills up the remainder of the space in the base of the cartridge bag which fits over it.

The charge is then secured into the case by means of a glazeboard disc, felt disc and wads, and a lid.

All information concerning the manufacture of the charge is contained on label on the lid of the cartridge.

ADAPTORS.—Metal adaptors are made of aluminium bronze, they are bored out to take a tube, and threaded on the outside to screw into the base of the cartridge case.

"FIXED AMMUNITION."—In the case of this ammunition the Projectile is secured to the mouth of the brass case by means of a groove round its base.

The charges are made up in a similar manner to other Q.F. charges.

The percussion cap, which is secured into the base of the cartridge, contains the percussion firing arrangements, which being struck by the striker ignites the powder igniter, which in turn ignites the charge; it thus takes the place of a tube and adaptor.

In the latest cartridges there is no powder igniter sewn into the end of the charge, but a percussion primer, which, in reality, combines cap and igniter, is screwed into the base of the cartridge case.

CASES.—Boxes, etc.

Outfit boxes.

Metal-lined cases

Small arm Ammunition boxes.

OUTFIT BOXES, are made of wood, lined with tin, made watertight and strengthened with battens and brass straps. The lid of the box is fastened by a frame, which engages in four metal bolts on the box itself, the frame being moved by a cam, which is worked by the metal key. A notch is made under the two corners of the lid, so that the handle of the key can be inserted and used as a lever for prising open the lid.

The 6in. box holds 4 cartridges stowed vertically.

4.7in.	,,	6	,,	horizontally.
4in.	,,	8	,,	,,
3in.	,,	4	,,	,,
15-pdr.	,,	22	,,	,,
13-pdr.	,,	4	,,	,,
12-pdr.	,,	8 or 10	,,	,,

Boxes for 6-pdr. and 3-pdr. Ammunition are made of wood. The lid works on hinges and is secured by a hasp and turn buckle.

They are lined with tin and made watertight.

The cartridges are stowed vertically, fitting into holes in the tin lining.

The 6-pdr. box holds 11 cartridges.

    3-pdr. ,,   16 ,,

Note:—Boxes for 3-pdr. Vickers (Semi Automatic) differ from 3-pdr. Hotchkiss in being slightly larger.

Note on Ammunition for 6-pdr. (Single tube) Hotchkiss Gun.

Special care is to be taken that only the ammunition provided for this gun is used, the charge for this gun being smaller than that for, ordinary 6-pdr. Hotchkiss.

The ammunition box is painted grey, with a black band round it and on the base of each cartridge are stencilled the words "single tube."

Metal Lined Cases are made of wood, lined with tin, and are fitted with a square hinged lid on top, and a bung under the lid.

The lid is secured by two gunmetal bolts which are screwed down by a *metal lined key*.

The following, amongst others, are stowed in metal-lined cases :—

    Rifle Ball Ammunition for boat work.

    Rockets.

    Very's lights.

S.A.A. Boxes are made of wood with a tin lining. There is a sliding wooden lid attatched to the box by a length of whip-cord. When supplied, the tin lining is hermetically sealed. To open the box :—Take out the split pin, slide back the lid, then tear off the cover of the lining according to the printed instructions.

Vent Sealing Tubes are specially constructed, as their name implies, to seal the vent against the rush of gas to the rear on firing.

Boxes of Electric tubes have the lettering on the lids in BLACK, those containing Percussion tubes in RED.

The action of the *Percussion Tube* is roughly as follows:—

The striker of the tube is forced inwards by the action of the striker of the gun, shearing its copper shearing wire, the point of the striker firing the cap on the point of the anvil, the flash from the cap igniting the powder in the tube, which in turn ignites the charge.

Percussion tubes have four notches cut in the rim, to distinguish them from Electric tubes.

In case of the older types of Percussion tubes, which have no notches, they can be distinguished from Electric tubes by the fact that the base of the Percussion tube is flush and has no metal contact disc.

The action of *the Electric tube* is roughly as follows:—

On contact being made, the current passes through an insulated brass pole in the centre of the tube, and escapes to "earth" across a wire bridge. This wire bridge fuzes and so ignites the powder in the tube and thence the charge.

T TUBES USED WITH THE 15-PDR. B.L. GUN.—DESCRIPTION.

T Tubes (Percussion) act in much the same way as the vent sealing percussion tubes. They are made in the shape of a T, the striker and detonator being at right angles to the powder magazine.

FRICTION TUBES are used for firing signal rockets from the rocket machine. They are made of quill or copper.

They are filled with powder, and carry a little detonating composition in the head, through which passes a roughened copper bar, fitted with an eye to which the tube lanyard is hooked.

On pulling the tube lanyard, the friction fires the detonating composition.

PROJECTILES.—The projectiles provided for D.A.M.S. are generally *Steel Common Shell.*

They are made of forged or cast steel and have a large cavity, a large bursting charge of powder, and are supplied fuzed with a base fuze. They are ready for action as supplied, and are painted black (except in the case of some 12-pdr. projectiles, see below).

HIGH EXPLOSIVE (H.E.) shell are sometimes supplied. They are distinguished by being painted yellow. They are made of forged steel, and have a large bursting charge of some form of high explosive.

They are supplied fuzed with a nose fuze, and the fuze is protected by a cap, secured by a pin. Both pin and cap have to be removed before entering the projectile in the gun.

PRACTICE PROJECTILES are solid and made of cast iron, or are common shell filled with salt.

MARKING OF PROJECTILES.

All solid shot have a white tip.

All shrapnel shell have a red tip.

A red band round the head denotes that the shell is filled, i.e., the bursting charge is in place.

A yellow band round the body denotes that the projectile is supplied for practice only.

All H.E. shells are painted yellow.

Steel common shell which can only be used in 12-pdr., 12 & 8-cwt. guns are painted grey.

Projectiles are marked "salt" when filled with salt for practice.

All shell having fuzes in them are marked with the word "Fuzed" in red.

(See Confidential Addenda 4).

TRANSPORT AND STOWAGE OF PROJECTILES.

Pointed common shell are issued and are to be transported as follows:—

4·7in. and below in boxes.

All other shell in bulk, except Fuzed Lyddite.

Base Fuzed Shell are never to be stowed "base to point," as there is a danger of the point of one projectile being driven into the fuze of the other.

DRIVING BANDS are made of copper, and grip the rifling of the gun as the projectile passes down the bore, thus giving it its turning motion.

They should be treated carefully, as if they become dented or otherwise damaged there is a tendency for gas to escape past the projectile, and inaccurate shooting will result.

FUZES.—BASE PERCUSSION TYPE, fitted to common shell. The action is roughly as follows:—

The pressure set upon firing drives in a spindle, releasing a retaining bolt, which allows a centrifugal bolt to fly out as the projectile revolves. As soon as the centrifugal bolt is clear, the detonating pellet is free to fly forward against a needle, and is only held back by a weak spring.

On striking, the detonating pellet flies forward, strikes the needle, and the flash ignites the magazine of the fuze and explodes the shell.

THE HOTCHKISS BASE PERCUSSION TYPE is fitted in 3 & 6-pdr. common shell, and the action is simpler.

THE DIRECT ACTION IMPACT FUZE.—This is a nose fuze, and is fitted to High Explosive Shell.

On impact the needle is crushed into the detonator, and explodes the projectile.

This type of fuze has not so many safety arrangements as the Base Fuzes and hence it is fitted with a safety cap, which has to be removed before firing.

303 RIFLE BALL AMMUNITION.—The charge is of cordite.

The bullet is of lead, with a nickel sheath.

FIREWORKS.

1-lb. *Signal Rocket* consists of a brown paper cylinder, filled with Rocket composition, the head containing stars. A special tube is fitted to fire it from, when the stick tail is used.

Method of firing with stick tail:—

Fit the stick tail to the rocket, taking care that the stick is pushed in till the catch secures it. Place rocket and stick in the tube.

Insert a friction tube in the lock, and hook on the firing lanyard. Pull the firing lanyard.

Method of firing with rope tail:—

Fit the rope tail, and hold the rocket so as to keep everything well clear of the back fire. Light at the bottom with a port fire, or a piece of slow match on the end of a rod. Hold on to the rocket until it begins to pull hard, then let go.

SOUND SIGNAL ROCKET.—It is similar in shape and construction to the above, but is fitted to take a guncotton cylinder in the head in lieu of the stars. The guncotton charge has a recess in it in which a detonator of Fulminate of Mercury fits.

To Fire the rocket:—

Place it on the stick as before. Open out the calico covering at the end. Take a guncotton primer and enlarge the recess in it with the *rectifier* and then place in the Fulminate detonator. Turn the whole rocket and stick upside down and place the guncotton primer and detonator in the top of the rocket, with the head of the detonator towards the rocket, and holding it here carefully, turn the rocket right side up again. Tie the calico covering over the guncotton. Place the rocket on the rocket machine and tear off the paper covering the safety fuze at the base of the rocket. Light the safety fuze.

NOTE:—If the detonator is dropped it will probably detonate with sufficient force to cause a nasty accident.

The *short light* burns from one and a half to two minutes. It consists of a brown paper cylinder filled with composition: one end of the cylinder is primed, the priming being covered with priming, the plug being held in place with a nail.

To ignite, tear off the paper disc, pull out the plug, and draw the pinned end lightly across the priming, holding the latter so that it points away from the body.

Very's Lights (Cartridges Signal 1-in.) are made up in cartridges and when fired throw up a bright ball, which is red, white or green. They are fired from a special pistol, and are for signalling purposes. These lights are distinguished by day by the colour of the cardboard at the end of the cartridge, and by night the rim of the base being :—

Milled all round in the red light.

Milled half round in the white light.

Plain all round in the green light.

To fire a Very's light half cock the pistol, pull out the catch below the barrel and open the pistol, insert the cartridge, close the pistol, then full cock and fire in the air. Before extracting the fired cartridge, half cock the pistol.

Slow Match burns at the rate of one yard in eight hours.

Common Port fires are paper cylinders filled with composition; they burn very fiercely from twelve to fifteen minutes, and can only be extinguished by cutting off the burning end.

They are useful for any incendiary purpose, i.e., firing rockets with rope tail, or igniting smoke boxes.

SMOKE BOXES.—

Type A. Method of igniting, precautions, &c.

Type E. Method of igniting, precautions, &c.

(See Confidential Addenda.)

IX.—HINTS ON SHOOTING.

The point of aim communicated to the Gunlayer should be some well-defined object, such as the conning tower at the water-line. It must be remembered that the point of aim is not necessarily the point of attack, and that fire can be distributed from bow to stern by alteration of the deflection without altering the point of aim.

Gunlayers must fully realise what is known as the "Firing interval," i.e., the interval of time between observing the crosswires "on" and the projectile leaving the muzzle, an average period of $\frac{1}{3}$rd of a second. What is required of the gunlayer is that the sights should be "On" when the projectile leaves the muzzle; this can only be obtained by being *steadied* on at the moment of pressing the trigger.

When firing with considerable motion on the ship, it must not be expected that the same degree of accuracy of aim can be obtained without a great alteration in the rate of fire, and hence latitude in the point of aim should be allowed, depending on the amount of motion; this latitude in no way obviates the necessity of the gun being steadied during the "Firing interval."

At the guns fitted with gunlayers' and trainers' telescopes, the sights are only converged for one range, and so at the other ranges both telescopes will not be on at once. The gunlayer should sing out "on" when he is on the point of aim, thus indicating to the trainer how far off the point of aim he should train to ensure the gunlayer being on. The gunlayer can then report "sights correct." The trainer must be able to keep his gun steadied on this point so that the gunlayer is at liberty to fire as soon as his sight is steadied for elevation.

To increase the rate of fire, the gunlayer and trainer should follow instinctively the operation of loading, so that just before the loading is completed, they are straining every nerve to have their gun steady by the time the report "Ready" is made.

The gunlayer should make a practice of reporting "good" or "bad" shot as he is taught in the school, and whether high, low, right, left as the case may be. This is especially important to the officer controlling a single gun, as an unreported bad shot may throw out the whole of his spotting.

X.—THE SUBMARINE.

The following general remarks on the submarine may be of interest.

The submarine is propelled on the surface by oil engines at a speed of from 16 to 18 knots, and under water by electric motors at a maximum speed of 10 knots.

She carries sufficient oil to last for several weeks, but the batteries which drive the electric motors under water have to be frequently recharged.

Under water she can only maintain her maximum speed for 4 hours, but she can proceed at 2 knots under water for about 18 hours.

Consequently she must come to the surface to recharge her batteries every 24 hours at least. She will probably do this at night, and remain under during the day.

The maximum distance a periscope is visible is about 2000 yards. So when on the "look-out"—up to 2000 yards, look out for periscopes, and beyond that for submarines on the surface.

On a clear day the submarine can see from 10—12000 yards through her periscope. She takes about one minute to dive from being on the surface, and when coming to the surface could get her gun into action in about two minutes.

The amount of ammunition she can carry is very large, but the number of torpedos is limited to about 10.

Consequently she cannot waste torpedos.

To make sure of hitting she must get within 1500 yards, and must be on or before the beam if she wishes to fire at a greater distance.

Very rough weather handicaps the submarine. She is continually liable to break surface and give herself away, and torpedos, if fired, will probably break surface and be seen.

www.ingramcontent.com/pod-product-compliance
Lightning Source LLC
Chambersburg PA
CBHW060221050426
42446CB00013B/3134